Dirt Cheap
40 Healthy Meal
Five Ingredients, Plu
by Alec So

Table of Contents:

Preface

40 Five Ingredient Paleo Meals:

- Seared Carne Asada
- Low and Slow Asian-Style Beef Ribs
- Portobello Garlic Burger
- Pork Carnitas
- BLT Lettuce Wraps
- Rosemary Pepper Encrusted Pot Roast
- Easy Crock Pot Maple Orange Pork Shoulder
- Vegetable Quiche
- Bacon-Ranch Meatloaf
- Ultimate Bacon Wrapped Meatloaf
- Chicken Apple Sausage and Spinach Skillet

Bonus: Paleo Breads & Taco Shells

- Paleo Backyard Hamburger Buns
- Grain-free Sandwich Bread
- Grain Free Taco Shells

Bonus: Deserts

- Quick Chocolate Cherry Dessert
- No-Heat Pumpkin Pie Pudding
- Chocolate Covered Frozen Banana and Peanut Butter Bites
- Paleo Watermelon Cake
- Simple Banana Bread Muffins
- Macadamia Chocolate Chip No-Heat Cookies
- Super Easy Chia Pudding
- Avocado Pear Popsicles
- Nectarine Kiwi Banana Baby Food Popsicles
- Mango Brûlée

Bonus: Condiments

- One Minute Mayo
- Garlic Aioli (garlic flavored, mayo like dip or spread)

- Dairy-Free Double Caramel Sauce
- Toasted Almond Hazelnut Butter
- Avocado Pesto Sauce
- Sugar Free Sweet and Sour Sauce
- Worcestershire Sauce
- Everyday Mustard
- Whole-grain mustard
- Cajun Creole Spicy Mustard
- Ketchup

Preface

I would like to personally thank you for purchasing my book Dirt Cheap Paleo, 40 Healthy Meals Under $2, Five Ingredients, Plus Bonus Recipes. I have made every effort to hunt down and test the very best paleo recipes anywhere for you to enjoy. Eating the right ingredients to live a healthy lifestyle can be demanding, especially when time and skill in the kitchen are short-handed. When I began this journey, I had only three requirements: simple, cheap and delicious.

First, the recipes had to be simple to make with less than five ingredients each. I'm the worst when it comes to keeping a stocked pantry or refrigerator and I never seem to have enough time to spend an hour or more each day in the kitchen, following a long and complicated recipe only to be faced with a mountain of dirty dishes to clean after eating. I do enjoy experimenting with long recipes on occasion but, for the most part, I just want to fuel my body with the best food I can find.

Second, since I know all too well what it's like to eat on a budget, each recipe had to be cheap to make. Lets face it, eating paleo can get expensive. Those of us following a paleo lifestyle have cut out all of the cheap drive-through fast foods, chips, sodas and candy. We no longer eat inexpensive potatoes, rice or bread fillers with every meal. Now we are eating natural meats, eggs, fresh vegetables, fruits and nuts. Fresh ingredients are more expensive. All of the recipes in this book can be prepared for around two dollars per serving when frugal shopping practices are followed and enough ingredients are purchased at one time to make four to six servings. Depending on where you shop and what you consider a serving size will dictate exactly how much each meal will cost you.

Third, and this is the most obvious, each recipe had to be delicious. I love eating good food just like anyone else, and when I eat, I want to eat food that tastes good.

When counting the ingredients for each recipe, I did not consider what I feel to be common kitchen ingredients such as cooking oils and spices. These items have always been a staple in my kitchen and I rarely run out of any of it. Only the main ingredients that a person would have to put on a short shopping list to buy are counted. Common ingredients are marked with an asterisk (*) throughout the book.

Since many of us enjoy other items such as (paleo) breads and condiments to compliment our meals and be truly satisfying, I have included a selection of such recipes as a bonus. To help with any cravings for sweets, there are also deliciously indulgent paleo recipes toward the back of the book.

I truly hope that you enjoy these recipes as much as I have. If you have enjoyed it, please take two or three minutes to go back and leave a review for this book. The more reviews I get, the more encouraged I am to write more books.

Thank you,

Alec Sommers

40 Five Ingredient Paleo Meals:

Bacon Avocado Spinach Omelet

Ingredients:

Bacon avocado spinach filling
1) 1 green onion, chopped
2) Large handful fresh spinach
3) Two strips cooked bacon, in pieces
4) 1/2 avocado, sliced
*) 2 tablespoons coconut or olive oil

Omelet
5) 2 to 3 large eggs
*) 2 tablespoons unsweetened coconut milk or almond milk
*) Salt and black pepper to taste

Directions:

Filling
1) Heat 1 tablespoon oil in an 8-inch pan, add green onions and bacon pieces. Saute briefly 1 minute.
2) Add spinach and cook 1/2 minute, add salt and pepper to taste, and set aside on a plate.

Omelet:
1) Crack the eggs into a bowl. Whisk in milk, salt, and pepper.
2) Heat 1 tablespoon oil in the pan over medium-low heat. When a drop of water sizzles when flicked on the surface, pour in the eggs.
3) Turn down the heat and cover. Do not stir. Just let the eggs cook for about 1 minute until bottom starts to set.
4) With a heat-resistant spatula, gently lift one side of the omelet without breaking it and allow the liquid egg to flow underneath into the bottom of the pan. Cook until it is just golden brown on the bottom and barely cooked on the top, about 2 minutes.

5) Add your filling by spooning it into bottom half of the circle of eggs. Top with avocado slices.
6) Gently slide the omelet onto a plate, filled side first, folding the other half over as you go.

For variety, replace the bacon and avocado with these variations:
1) Mushroom Watercress – 1/2 cup fresh sliced mushrooms, sautéed in garlic and olive oil, a handful of fresh watercress, slightly wilted.
2) Turkey Gobbler – 1/4 cup diced turkey meat, 2 tablespoons diced cooked bacon, 2 tablespoons chopped green onion.
3) Wild Salmon and Green Onion – Sauté 1 diced green onion with 3 ounces wild salmon. Serve with grass-fed goat cheese.
4) Wild Mushrooms and Asparagus – Sauté 1/4 cup raw mushrooms in garlic and coconut oil. Add four spears asparagus. Steam until tender. Serve with parsley.

Chorizo Butternut Squash Hash

Ingredients:
1) 1 small butternut squash, peeled and diced small (208 grams)
2) ½ yellow onion, finely diced
3) ½ pound chorizo
4) salt and pepper, to taste
5) 5 eggs

Directions:
1) Place a cast iron skillet or pan over medium heat. Add butternut squash and onion.
2) After cooking the butternut squash on all sides for about 5-8 minutes or until squash is soft, add chorizo. Break up chorizo into small pieces and cook until completely cooked through. Add a bit of salt and pepper.
3) Use a spoon to press in 5 little crevices. Crack eggs into the crevices. Place a lid over the pan and cook until eggs are cooked to over easy (or to preference), about 3-4 minutes.

Slow-cooker (Crock-Pot®) Salsa Verde Chicken

Ingredients:
1) 6 boneless, skinless chicken breasts
2) 2 cups salsa verde
3) 1 bottle gluten free beer (or chicken broth)
4) 2 teaspoons cumin
5) 1 jalapeño, stem removed and diced, leaving the seeds in for extra heat (optional)
*) Sea salt and black pepper to taste

Directions:
1) Add chicken to Crock-Pot®
2) Top with salsa verde and beer
3) Sprinkle with cumin and season with a few generous pinches of salt and a pinch of pepper
4) Use a pair of tons or a spoon to turn the chicken so that both sides are coated
5) Cover and cook for 3-4 hours on high heat, or 7-8 hours on low heat
6) Chicken is ready when it easily shreds with a fork. Shred the chicken in the slow cooker, and toss with the juices
7) Remove with a slotted spoon and serve warm. (can be stored in a sealed container in the refrigerator for up to 5 days, or in the freezer for up to 3 months

Zesty Mustard Baked Chicken Thighs

Ingredients:
1) 1.5 pound Boneless Skinless Chicken thighs (4-6)
2) ½ cup cajun creole mustard (or ZATARAIN'S® Creole Mustard any other whole grain spicy mustard)
3) ¼ cup 100% pure maple syrup
4) 2 tablespoons paleo Worcestershire sauce
5) 1 Tablespoon oregano

Directions:
1) Preheat oven to 450°F
2) Line a 9x9 baking dish with foil.

3) Place chicken thighs in the baking dish.
4) In a separate bowl, stir together mustard, syrup, Worcestershire sauce and oregano.
5) Pour over chicken thighs, making sure they are entirely covered.
6) Bake, uncovered, for 40 minutes.
7) Serve with your favorite veggies

Cajun Bacon Wrapped Shrimp

Ingredients:
1) 8 jumbo shrimp, peeled and deveined, leaving tails on
2) 8 slices bacon
3) ZATARAIN'S® Creole Seasoning (as needed)

Directions:
1) Preheat oven to 450°F.
2) Line baking pan with foil. Place wire baking rack in pan. (or line pan with crumpled aluminum foil)
3) Wrap each shrimp with 1 slice of bacon, held together with a toothpick
4) Place shrimp on rack. Lightly sprinkle both sides with Creole Seasoning. Let stand 15 minutes.
5) Bake 15 to 20 minutes or until bacon is crisp around the edges and shrimp turn pink. Serve warm.

Tuna Stuffed Recovery Potatoes

Ingredients:
1) 8 potatoes of your choice
2) 2 eggs
3) 1 cup of chopped pickles
4) 28 ounces of tuna, drained
5) 1/2 cup ghee or olive oil
Salt & Pepper

Directions:
1) Preheat your oven to 400 degrees.

2) Add a drop or two of oil to the potato skin and rub it in. Then sprinkle with salt.

3) Cook the potatoes for 50-60 minutes, until tender in the middle when you insert a fork.

4) Remove the potatoes from the oven, cut the potatoes in half to them cool down.

5) Let the potatoes cool about 10 minutes. Once cooled, take a spoon and remove the flesh from the skins, leaving just a small amount on the edges to maintain the shape, like a bowl. Add flesh to a large bowl.

6) Chop up your pickles into small cubes.

7) Drain tuna and add it to potato flesh. Mix thoroughly.

8) Add pickles and mix thoroughly once again.

9) Add 1/2 cup of ghee or olive oil, and 2 eggs. Mix until incorporated.

10) Evenly distribute the mixture into the 8 potato halves.

11) Bake in the oven at 400 for an additional 15 minutes, until starting to brown on the tops.

Easy Dutch Oven Braised Cabbage

Ingredients:
1) 1 large head of cabbage
2) 1 medium onion, diced
3) 2 tablespoons cooking oil
4) 1 cup of chicken or beef stock
5) 1/2 tablespoon of salt

Directions:
1) Preheat oven to 375 degrees. Put dutch oven on the stove and turn on heat to medium-high.

2) Chop onion, then add cooking oil to the pan. Throw in onions, and stir.

3) Add half of salt to onions and cook for 8-10 minutes, until starting to be translucent and soft.

4) While onions are cooking, chop cabbage into quarters, take out the core, and then slice into ribbons. You could throw in the food processor if you prefer.

5) After the onions have cooked, add to cabbage. It will be very full at this point! Drizzle your 1 cup of stock on top, and your remaining salt.

6) Put the lid on and pop in the oven for 60 minutes, stirring at the half way point and taking the lid off for the last 30 minutes.

Maple Nut Roasted Butternut Squash

Ingredients:
1) 2 pounds of butternut squash, peeled and cubed
2) 2 tablespoons ghee or butter, or coconut oil
3) 2 tablespoons maple syrup
4) 1/2 cup of nuts, your choice (almonds are great!)
5) 1/4 teaspoon salt

Directions:
1) Preheat oven to 400 degrees.
2) In a 9x13 pan, or a rimmed baking with silicone mat or parchment paper, add your chopped butternut squash.
3) In a small bowl, mix together 2 tablespoons of ghee and 2 tablespoons of maple syrup. Stir well.
4) Pour the liquid mixture on top of your squash. Mix with your hands to ensure everything is evenly covered.
5) In a food processor or blender, grind the 1/2 cup of nuts down until small pieces, almost like flour.
6) Spread the ground nuts evenly over your squash. Sprinkle with salt.
7) Bake for 30-35 minutes, until tender to your liking.

Zucchini Noodles with Sautéed Shrimp

Ingredients:
1) 4 med zucchini, made into noodles with a spiralizer
2) 2 Tbsp coconut oil
3) 6 cloves fresh garlic, minced
4) 24 lg pre-cooked shrimp, rinsed and tails removed
5) 2 pkg (6 c total) grape tomatoes, halved

*) ⅓ c fresh basil, chopped
*) Sea salt and ground pepper

Directions:
1) Cut zucchini into curly noodles using a spiralizer or spiral slicer, and set aside in a large glass bowl.
2) In a large wok or skillet, heat cooking fat over low to medium heat.
3) Add garlic and cook until softened, about 5 minutes.
4) Turn the heat up to medium and add shrimp to the wok. Cook, stirring occasionally, for 5 minutes.
5) Add tomatoes and continue to stir, cooking for 10 more minutes.
6) Add zucchini noodles and basil to the wok, and cook until noodles have softened, about 7 minutes.
7) Sprinkle with salt and pepper. Garnish with freshly chopped basil, if desired.

Paleo Pancakes

Ingredients:
1) 1 egg
2) 1 ripe banana
3) Strawberries (or any berries for the topping)
4) Coconut oil (as needed)
*) Pinch of salt
*) Cinnamon

Directions:
1) Blend banana and egg
2) Add cinnamon and salt
3) Cook on skillet in coconut oil until slightly brown on each side
4) Garnish with berries

Roasted Carrot Fries with Garlic Aioli

Ingredients: (for Carrot Fries):
1) Peeled and cut carrots

2) Coconut oil
3) Salt/pepper

Directions:
1) Heat oven to 425 degrees
2) In a bowl, toss carrots with coconut oil, salt, and pepper
3) Place on baking sheet and cook for 30 min flipping over halfway through

Ingredients: (for Garlic Aioli):
1) 2 garlic cloves
2) 2 egg yolks
3) ½ to ¾ cup olive oil (depending on desired thickness)
4) Juice of ½ lemon
5) Pinch of salt

Directions:
1) Combine all Ingredients: except olive oil in a food processor or blender
2) Slowly add olive oil until the sauce is fairly thick
3. Dip with carrot fries

Sweet Potato Balls

Ingredients:
1) 5-6 Medium sized Sweet Potatoes
2) ½ to ¾ cup coconut milk
3) 1/8 cup unsweetened shredded coconut

Directions:
1) Boil potatoes until you can stick a chopstick all the way through
2) Peel potatoes
3) Mash potatoes in a bowl or food processor until softened
4) Mix in coconut milk and shredded coconut
5) Use a melon scooper to scoop and roll into balls

Zucchini Noodles & Meatballs

Ingredients:
1) 4 med zucchini, made into noodles with a spiralizer
2) ½ lb. ground beef
3) 1 can or bottle marinara sauce
4) 1 tbsp. Italian seasoning
5) 5 cloves of garlic (minced)

Directions:
1) Make small balls with beef
2) Heat skillet onto medium high and place meatballs on skillet
3) Move around until the balls are brown on all sides
4) Add garlic and sauté until fragrant
5) Add marinara sauce and Italian seasonings to skillet and bring to a boil
6) Reduce heat and let simmer, adjust seasonings to taste.
7) Place zucchini in a microwave safe bowl and cover. Cook for 3 to 4 min or until tender
9. Place zucchini noodles in bowl and top with sauce.

Paleo Waffles

Ingredients:
1) 4 pastured eggs
2) 1 ripe banana
3) 1 Tbsp coconut flour (optional: cinnamon, pumpkin pie spice, or vanilla)

Directions:
1) Put all Ingredients: in a blender
2) Pour into a hot waffle iron and cook until done
3) Top with 100% pure maple syrup, grass-fed butter and fresh fruit

Paleo Oatmeal with Coconut

Ingredients:
1) 1/2 cup full-fat canned coconut milk PLUS 1/4 cup water OR 3/4

cup homemade coconut milk OR 3/4 cup water
2) 3 Tbs. coconut flour
3) 2 Tbs. finely shredded coconut
4) 1 pastured egg (or 1/2 banana, mashed for egg free option)
5) Berry toppings of your choice

Directions:
1)In a small saucepan, mix together the liquid, coconut flour and shredded coconut.
2) Bring to a boil (mixture will be thick), cover, reduce heat to low, and simmer for 2-3 minutes. Stir halfway through.
3) Remove saucepan from heat, crack the egg into the saucepan and whisk quickly to prevent the egg from scrambling.
4) Return to the heat and stir until thickened, about 2 minutes.
Note: For the egg free version, follow the directions above but don't add the egg. Instead, whisk in the mashed banana and stir briefly.

Grain Free Pumpkin Pancakes

Ingredients:
1) 2 eggs
2) ¼ cup pumpkin puree
3) ⅛ tsp. cinnamon
4) Coconut oil for the pan
5) Top with 100% pure maple syrup, grass-fed butter and fresh fruit

Directions:
1) Warm a cast iron pan over medium high heat
2) Whisk together the eggs, pumpkin puree, and cinnamon
3) Add about a tablespoon of coconut oil to the hot pan and swirl to cover the bottom of the pan.
4) Use about two tablespoons of batter for each pancake. They flip best when the pancakes are small
5) Cook until golden on the bottom and slightly opaque in the center and around the edges
6) Flip, brown on the other side, and serve
7) Makes about 8 small pancakes

Baked Eggs in Prosciutto-Filled Portobello Mushroom Caps

Ingredients:
1) 4 eggs (farm fresh if available)
2) 4 medium portobello mushroom caps
3) 4 slices of prosciutto
4) black pepper to taste
5) fresh herbs of choice
*) Olive oil (as needed)

Directions:
1) Clean the portobello mushroom caps with a damp cloth, remove the stem and scrape out the gills so you have a well deep enough for the egg
2) Rub a little bit of olive oil on the outside of the mushroom to help it cook and keep it from sticking to the pan
3) Arrange the caps on a baking sheet
4) Place one slice of prosciutto inside each mushroom cap
5) Crack each egg into a small bowl and then carefully slide it onto a prosciutto-filled mushroom cap
6) Sprinkle with black pepper and fresh herbs
7) CAREFULLY place the baking pan into the pre-heated 375 degree F oven and bake for 20-30 minutes. The amount of time required depends on how thick your mushrooms are and how done you like your eggs. Serves two.

Bacon Brussel Sprouts Slaw

Ingredients:
1) ½ pound bacon, diced
2) 16 ounces brussel sprouts, shredded
3) ½ red onion, diced
4) 2 teaspoons apple cider vinegar
5) 2-3 precooked sausages (I used game sausage, but use any kind you like)
*) ¼ teaspoon garlic powder
*) salt and pepper, to taste

Directions:
1) Place a dutch oven over medium heat.
2) Add bacon and cook until crispy. Remove with a slotted spoon and place on a paper towel lined plate.
3) Add brussel sprouts, onion and apple cider vinegar to the rendered bacon fat in the dutch oven. Sprinkle with salt and pepper and a bit of garlic powder.
4) Cook on low to medium for about 10 minutes, stirring every couple minutes.
5) Once brussel sprouts become soft, add sausage and bacon to dutch oven, mix, and cook for no more than than 5 minutes, until sausage is hot.
6) Sprinkle with a bit more salt, if desired, before serving.

Maple Roasted Chicken with Sweet Potatoes

Ingredients:
1) 2-4 chicken thighs or breasts. bone-in/skin-on
2) 2 large sweet potatoes
3) 1 yellow onion
4) 3 tbsp 100% pure maple syrup
5) 8 sprigs fresh thyme
*) 2 tbsp olive oil
*) 3/4 tsp salt, plus more to taste
*) 1/4 tsp pepper, plus more to taste

Directions:
1) Preheat oven to 400 degrees
2) Peel sweet potatoes and chop into 1 inch thick pieces (smaller rounds can be left whole, cut larger ones in half)
3) Roughly chop up onion into about 1 inch pieces
4) In a large baking dish, toss the potatoes, onions, chicken, olive oil, maple syrup, salt, and pepper together
5) Position chicken skin-side down on the bottom of pan so that it will cook in the liquid and stay moist
6) Top with thyme sprigs and place on center rack in oven
7) Bake about 40 minutes, uncovered, stirring half way through (the

thyme leaves should begin to fall off as it cooks)

8) Once chicken is cooked, turn the chicken skin side up, atop the veggies

9) Broil for a few minutes, until golden brown and crispy

10)Serve chicken topped with potatoes, onions and sauce. Sprinkle with a little salt, pepper, and fresh thyme leaves as desired.

Shrimp Scampi with Zucchini Noodles

Ingredients:
1) 2 lbs large wild shrimp, peeled and deveined
2) 4 Tbsp butter
3) 3 cloves garlic, minced
4) 2 organic lemons
5) 3 medium zucchini, cut into zucchini noodles with a spiral slicer or julienne peeler
*) Red pepper flakes, to taste

Directions:
1) Precook the zucchini noodles by lightly steaming them until almost tender.
2) Heat 2 Tbsp of butter in a large skillet or medium high heat
3) Add the garlic and stir into the butter.
4) Add the shrimp and sear for 1-2 minutes per side.
5) Add the lemon juice and salt & pepper to taste
6) Add the zucchini noodles and toss in the sauce.
7) Serve with red pepper flakes for a kick

Paleo Lunch Wraps

Ingredients:
1) 3 large eggs
2) 2 tablespoons arrowroot powder (substitute with almond powder or coconut flour)
3) Large handful parsley or salad greens
*) 2 pinches of sea salt
*) 1 teaspoon fresh herbs such as tarragon, thyme or basil (optional)

Directions:
Make the Wraps
1) Add all Ingredients: to any blender: eggs, arrowroot, salt, parsley or greens, herbs. Blend well until greens are as liquefied as possible.
2) Preheat an 8-inch non-stick pan over medium low heat. Brush the pan well with a bit of olive oil before making each wrap. Heat the pan until a drop of water sizzles.
3) Use 1/4 cup batter for each wrap. The first wrap is a test for the batter and the heat level, so it might not be perfect - do not be alarmed. It is important for the batter to be quite thin. If your veggies are thick, you may need to thin the batter with a little water. Adjust the heat if necessary and your next few wraps should be just fine.
4) Pour the batter into the pan and twirl it around to make a circular form. Watch it cook, and when it begins to firm up and dry out on the sides, use a spatula to gently release the edges and bottom. When the entire wrap can pull away from the pan, flip it over gently with your fingers. Cook briefly on the second side. It should still be moist, not overcooked. If it's too dry it will be brittle and harder to roll. Slip it out of the pan onto a plate. Repeat until all the wraps are cooked. Cover with a dry towel.
5) Fill with ingredient you want. Try with Bacon Brussel Sprout Slaw. 1 and 1/2 to 2 cups filling for 6 wraps.

Thai Chicken Satay

Ingredients:
1) 1 cup coconut milk
2) 3 cloves garlic, grated
3) 1 tbsp curry powder
4) 1-2 tsp, fresh ginger, grated
5) 2.5 lbs chicken tenders
*) 1 tsp sea salt

Directions:
1) Combine coconut milk, ginger, curry powder and salt in a mixing bowl. Mix until evenly combined
2) Marinate chicken with mixture for 2-4 hours

3) Soak wooden skewers for a minimum of one hour, prior to grilling
4) Preheat grill to high heat (can also be broiled in the oven)
5) Skewer chicken tenders with pre-soaked wooden skewers
6) Grill over medium heat (or broil) for 8-12 minutes, turning as necessary to cook evenly

Crock-Pot® Kahlua Pig

Ingredients:
1) 5 pound Boston butt roast (bone-in or out—it doesn't matter)
2) 3 slices of bacon
3) 1½ tablespoons coarse sea salt or 1 tablespoon of fine sea salt. (Note: use ¾ teaspoon of medium-coarse salt for every 1 pound of meat or about half that amount for fine salt)
4) 5 peeled garlic cloves

Directions:
1) Line the Crock-Pot® with 3 slices of bacon
2) Use a knife to remove the skin from the roast (optional)
3) Cut slits into the meat and tuck in garlic cloves
4) Salt pork all over
5) Place pork on top of bacon, skin side up.
6) Cooked the roast on low for about 16 hours. (Note: newer slow cookers are hotter and may only require 9-12 hours on the low setting.) Do not add any liquid!
7) When the pork is finished cooking, remove from the Crock-Pot® and shred the meat with two forks
8) Check for proper seasoning and add a little cooking liquid from the bottom of the pot as needed. (Don't add too much of the cooking liquid, it will be too salty)

Crock-Pot® Baby Back Ribs

Ingredients:
1) 3 pounds baby back ribs, trimmed
2) 1 (18 ounce) bottle paleo barbecue sauce
3) 1/2 onion, sliced

4) 1 clove garlic, minced
*) 1/2 cup water
*) Sea salt and ground black pepper, to taste

Directions:
1) Season ribs with salt and pepper
2) Pour water into slow cooker. Layer the ribs into the slow cooker. Top the ribs with onion and garlic
3) Cook on High for 4 hours (or Low for 8 hours, Low is better)
4) Preheat oven to 375 degrees F (190 degrees C)
5) Transfer ribs to a baking sheet. Discard onion and garlic. Coat ribs with barbecue sauce
6) Bake in preheated oven until the sauce caramelizes and sticks to the meat, 10 to 15 minutes

Lemon Pepper Chicken Burgers

Ingredients:
1) 1lb Ground Chicken
2) 2-3 Diced Scallions
3) 1 tsp lemon pepper seasoning
4) 1 tsp Minced Garlic
5) Fresh Squeezed Juice from 1/2 a Lemon
*) Sea salt to taste

Directions:
1) Put all Ingredients: in a bowl and mix together by hand, careful not to overmix
2) Hand-pat into patties
3) Grill or broil until done, turning once
4) Serve by itself with veggies, wrapped in a lettuce wrap or on your favorite paleo bread.

Pork Apple Hash

Ingredients:
1) 2 pounds of ground pork or sausage
2) 3 apples, cored and diced

3) 3 large onions, chopped (6 cups)
4) 1 large sweet potato, chopped (12 ounces)

Directions:
1) Heat up a large skillet over medium-high heat, add your pork and cook until brown.
2) While the pork is cooking, chop up the apples, onions and sweet potato into bite-sized pieces. Try to make them all the same size to aid with even cooking.
3) Once the pork is cooked, add in all chopped vegetables and fruit.
4) Cook for 20-30 minutes, stirring often, until everything is tender and cooked thoroughly.
5) Serve with your favorite paleo bread

Hearty Shepard's Pie with Cauliflower Topping
Ingredients:
1) 2 pounds of ground beef or lamb
2) 2 pounds of carrots, sliced
3) 3 onions, diced
4) 1-2 large heads of cauliflower or bags of cauliflower florets
5) 2 tablespoons of spices of your choice

Directions:
1) Brown ground meat in the largest skillet you have, over medium-high heat until cooked.
2) Drain at least 1/4 to 1/2 cup of the oil into a cup to use for your mashed cauliflower. Leave the rest of the oil in the pan to help cook the vegetables.
3) Once you've drained the oil, add in onions and carrots. Cook these for 25-30 minutes over medium-high heat until they are soft and cooked thoroughly.
4) While the carrots and onions are cooking with the meat, start on the cauliflower. Chop up cauliflower heads to just leave the florets, then add to a large bowl. If using a bag, just add the bag's contents to a large bowl. Add about a tablespoon of water and microwave on high for 6-10 minutes, until soft.
5) Add the cooked cauliflower to a food processor.
6) For each batch of cauliflower, do the following: add in half of the

cauliflower for the batch to the food processor. Then add in oil (if you divided this into two batches, only add half the oil). Puree until smooth, then add in the other half of your cauliflower and puree.

7) Add the pureed cauliflower to a large bowl. Season with salt and pepper until you like how it tastes.

8) Preheat oven to 400 degrees

9) Once the onions and carrots are cooked, add all the spices to the dish. Stir to incorporate, and then add the mixture to a large casserole dish or 9x13 pan.

10) Spread the mashed cauliflower on top of the meat mixture. Spread it into an even layer.

11) Cook in the oven at 400 degrees for 45-60 minutes, until the top is brown and bubbly.

12) Once cooked, let rest for 10 minutes before serving

Plum-flavored Eggplant Casserole

Ingredients:

1) 3 pounds of peeled, cubed eggplant (about 4-5 large eggplants whole)

2) 2 pounds of ground beef, turkey, pork or chicken

3) 4 cups of tomato sauce (2 cans of 15oz)

4) 3/4 cup of prunes, chopped after measuring (about 20 prunes)

5) 1/2 cup of almond flour

Directions:

1) Brown ground meat on medium heat

2) Place peeled and diced eggplant in a colander or a large bowl, and sprinkle with a small amount of salt. This will help with some of the bitterness

3) Once the meat has browned, strain it from the pan, leaving some oil in the pan to assist in cooking the eggplant

4) Add the eggplant to the pan with your reserved oil from the ground meat. Continue to cook on medium heat, stirring occasionally, for 10-15 minutes, until the eggplant has softened completely

5) While the eggplant is cooking, add 1 can of tomato sauce and the prunes into a food processor. Puree until smooth.

6) Once the eggplant has finished cooking, stir in tomato mixture and add the 1 additional can of tomato sauce to the mixture.
7) Add in ground beef, and stir to incorporate
8) Transfer everything into a large 9x13 pan and spread evenly
9) Sprinkle almond flour on top of the casserole as evenly as possible
9) Cook in the oven at 350 degrees for 30-40 minutes until bubbly

Spinach Stuffed Flank Steak

Ingredients:
1) 1½ lb. flank steak
2) 6 oz. spinach, chopped
3) 1 bell pepper, seeds removed and chopped
4) 1 tomato, diced
5) 2 garlic cloves, minced
*) 1 tablespoon almond oil or walnut oil
*) Sea salt and freshly ground black pepper
*) Any other herbs of choice

Directions:
1) Preheat your oven to 425 F.
2) Lay the steak on a flat surface. Using a sharp knife held parallel to the cutting board, slice horizontally through the steak, stopping just short of the far side so you can open it up like a book.
3) Flatten the steak to an even thickness using a rolling pin or meat hammer.
4) Heat some cooking fat in a skillet placed over a medium heat, add the garlic, and cook for 1 minute.
5) Add all the spinach, season to taste, and cook for 2 minutes or until the spinach is wilted.
6) Season the steak to taste.
7) In bowl combine the tomato, bell pepper, and spinach mixture.
8) Press the filling all over the top of the steak.
9) Roll up the steak to enclose the filling. If any falls out the ends, tuck it back in.
10) Tie the steak into its rolled shape with cotton twine.
11) Roast the steak for 30 to 35 minutes; then finish it up by broiling

for 5 minutes.

12) Let the meat rest for a few minutes. Remove the twine, slice, and serve.

Seared Carne Asada

Ingredients:

1) 2 lb. sirloin steak
2) 2 cloves garlic, minced
3) Juice of 1 lime
*) 1 tablespoon almond oil or walnut oil
*) 1 tsp. dried oregano
*) 1 tbsp. paprika
*) 1 tbsp. powdered ancho chile or chili powder
*) ½ tsp. ground cumin
*) Sea salt and freshly ground black pepper to taste

Directions:

1) In a small bowl, combine the garlic, oregano, paprika, cumin, ancho chile, and season with salt and pepper to taste
2) Rub the meat with the lime juice
3) Rub the seasonings into the meat
4) Let it marinate in the refrigerator at least 2 hours (overnight is better)
5) Remove from the refrigerator and leave at room temperature another 30 minutes
6) Heat oil in a skillet over medium-high heat and sear the sirloin 3 to 4 minutes on each side, or until it reaches your desired doneness. Slice thin.

Low and Slow Asian-Style Beef Ribs

Ingredients:

1) 4 lb beef ribs
2) ¼ cup coconut aminos
3) 1 small bunch green onions, sliced
4) 6 garlic cloves, minced
*) 1 tablespoon fresh ginger, minced (or 1 teaspoon ground ginger)

*) 1 tablespoon fresh red chili, seeded and minced (or 1 teaspoon red chili flakes)
*) 1 1/2 cups water
*) 2 tablespoon raw honey (optional)

Directions:
1) In a bowl combine the coconut aminos, ginger, garlic, red chili, green onions, water, and honey (if using)
2) Place ribs in Crock-Pot® and pour the sauce on top
3) Cover and cook on low heat for 7 to 8 hours, or until the ribs are tender

Portobello Garlic Burger

Ingredients:
1) 3lbs of ground beef (not too lean if you want a very flavorful patty)
2) 3 eggs
3) 4 cloves garlic, minced and divided
4) 6-8 large Portabello mushrooms
*) A few tablespoons of olive oil (the amount will depend on how large your mushrooms are, start with a little then add more as needed)
*) 2 cloves garlic, minced
*) Sea salt and freshly ground black pepper to taste

Directions:
1) Place the ground beef in a large bowl and add the eggs. Combine until the eggs are evenly mixed through
2) Mix in the garlic and season with salt and pepper
3) Form 6 to 8 patties that are slightly smaller than the mushroom caps so they can fit on top once cooked
4) Place on a preheated grill and cook each side for about 5-7 minutes (the time it takes will depend on the temperature of your grill). Oven broiler can also be used.
5) Rinse the mushrooms and pat them dry.
6) Remove the mushroom stems. Coat the caps in olive oil and then season with salt and pepper. Do not let the oil penetrate for long or

the mushrooms will start to get soggy.

7) Place on the preheated grill and cook on each side for about 5-7 minutes. Oven broiler can also be used.

8) Stack the patties on top of the mushroom cap "bun" and add any toppings you desire.

Pork Carnitas

Ingredients:
1) 4 pound boneless pork butt, cut into 2 inch cubes
2) 1 medium orange, juiced, and keep the spent halves
3) 1 onion, peeled and quartered
4) 6 garlic cloves, peeled
5) 2 tbsp. fresh lime juice
*) 2 tsp. ground cumin
*) 2 bay leaves
*) 1 tsp. dried oregano
*) 2 cups of water

Directions:
1) Preheat your oven to 300 F.
2) Combine all the Ingredients: in a Dutch oven, and bring the mixture, uncovered, to a simmer over a medium-high heat.
3) Cover and transfer to the pre-heated oven.
4) Cook for 1.5 – 2 hours or until the meat falls apart.
5) Remove the pot from the oven and set the oven to broil.
6) Remove the meat from the pan and place on a baking sheet.
7) Discard everything from the Dutch oven except for the liquid.
8) Pour the liquid in a saucepan, bring to a boil, and simmer for 20 to 25 minutes or until the liquid becomes thick.
9) Pour the sauce over the meat and mix until well coated.
10) Place the pork in the oven and broil for 8 to 10 minutes, turning once
11) Serve immediately

BLT Lettuce Wraps

Ingredients:
1) 4 slices bacon
2) 1 tomato, sliced thin
3) 2 whole romaine leaves
4) 2 tablespoons paleo mayonnaise
5) Sea salt and fresh ground pepper to taste

Directions:
1) Spread each lettuce leaf with a generous portion of mayo.
2) Sprinkle with salt & pepper
3) Top with two strips of bacon, then a layer of sliced tomatoes, and two more slices of bacon.

Rosemary Pepper Encrusted Pot Roast

Ingredients:
1) Large cut of beef that is suitable for a pot roast and will fit in your crock pot
2) Sprig fresh rosemary
3) 2-3 carrots, cut into large chunks
4) 1 medium onion, cut into quarters
5) 2 large potatoes, cut into large chunks
*) Sea salt and fresh ground black pepper

Directions:
1) Pat the roast dry with a paper towel. Coat with sea salt and pepper on all sides and press firmly into meat.
2) Sear roast over medium heat, preferably in a cast iron skillet (any skillet will do though), on all sides to seal in the juices and makes the roast a deep golden brown.
3) Add roast to a crock pot along with a sprig of rosemary. Set to Low and let cook for at least 8 hours. The longer you let this meat cook, the more tender and juicy it will be.
4) Add carrots, onion and potatoes during the last two hours of cooking

Easy Crock Pot Maple Orange Pork Shoulder

Ingredients:
1) 2.5-3lbs. pork shoulder, cut into several big chunks
2) 1/2 cup of fresh squeezed orange juice
3) 1 apple, peeled and chopped
4) 1 tablespoon 100% pure maple syrup
*) 1/2 teaspoon dried sage
*) 1 teaspoon sea salt and 1/2 teaspoon black pepper, to taste

Directions:
1) Rub the pork with the salt, pepper and sage. Place it in the slow cooker.
2) Add the apples, orange juice and maple syrup.
3) Cook on low for 6 hours. Once it is cooked, use 2 forks to pull the pork apart.

Vegetable Quiche

Ingredients:
1) 8-10 Stalks of asparagus chopped
2) Big handful of fresh spinach or 1 cup frozen
3) 1 cup Frozen onions & peppers
4) 8 Eggs
5) 2 tablespoons paleo mayonnaise
*) 2 tablespoons olive oil (bacon fat is better)
*) 1 teaspoon marjoram
*) 1 teaspoon sea salt and 1 teaspoon black pepper, to taste

Directions:
1) Sauté asparagus, onions & peppers in olive oil or bacon fat in a cast iron skillet or oven friendly frying pan
2) Add the spinach
3) Beat eggs, spices and 2 tablespoons of mayonnaise together well
4) fold egg mixture into skillet
5) Bake in oven at 375 for 15-20 minutes

Bacon-Ranch Meatloaf

Ingredients:
1) 2 lbs ground beef
2) 1/2 cup plus 1/4 cup chopped cooked bacon
3) 2 tbsp coconut flour
4) 1 egg
5) 2 cloves garlic, minced
*) 1 tbsp dried parsley
*) 1 tsp dried dill
*) 1 tsp onion powder
*) 1 teaspoon sea salt
*) 1/2 tsp black pepper
*) Coconut oil for greasing the pan, if needed.

Directions:
1) Preheat the oven to 375°F (190°C)
2) Combine all of the Ingredients: above except for the coconut oil and a quarter cup of the cooked chopped bacon by hand. 3) Once evenly combined shape into a loaf and place on a baking sheet or tuck into a bread loaf pan lightly greased with oil
4) Top the loaf with the remaining quarter cup of cooked chopped bacon. It's a good idea to press the bacon into the loaf just a bit so that it stays in place.
5) Bake at 375°C (190°C) for about an hour or until the internal temperature at the center of the loaf reaches 160°F (71°C).
6) Remove the meatloaf from the oven at 155°F and allow it to rest for 5 to 10 minutes before slicing and serving.

Ultimate Bacon Wrapped Meatloaf

Ingredients:
1) 1 pound of bacon (divided; one quarter diced, the rest kept in strips)
2) 2 pounds ground beef
3) 1 cup diced green peppers (deveined and deseeded)
4) 2 medium onion, diced
5) 2 eggs, lightly beaten
*) 2 tablespoons garlic powder

*) 1 teaspoon sea salt and 1 teaspoon black pepper, to taste

Directions:
1) Preheat oven to 480 degrees F (make sure its hot)
2) Sauté diced bacon in a hot frying pan. Add the diced onions, salt and black pepper, and keep frying until the onion softens a bit. Allow to cool.
3) Using your hands, mix ground beef, bacon/onion mixture, eggs, green peppers, garlic powder and salt & pepper in a large bowl thoroughly
3) Line a large loaf tin with the bacon strips allowing the ends hang out over the edges and each strip overlapping the previous one. Keep three to four strips aside for later.
4) Form the meat mixture into a loaf put it pan on top of the bacon. Press down on it to make sure there are no air pockets inside the meat loaf.
6) Place the remaining bacon strips overlapping lengthwise on top of the meat mixture, then fold over all the ends that were left hanging over.
7) Put in oven and immediately turn down the heat to 350F
8) Bake for 45 minutes, then remove from oven.
9) Drain oil from pan, then flip pan over onto a baking tray, removing the pan from the loaf.
10)Put it back in the oven for 10-15 minutes until the bacon is a crispy golden brown.

Chicken Apple Sausage and Spinach Skillet

Ingredients:
1) 1 Package Chicken Apple Sausage, sliced
2) 5 garlic cloves, chopped
3) 1 package grape tomatoes, chopped in half
4) 2 big handfuls fresh spinach (or as much as you like, it will cook down)
*) Coconut Oil – about 1 tablespoon

Directions:
1) Heat coconut oil on medium heat in a non-stick pan. Saute the

sausage and garlic together in the oil until they start to brown.

2) Add grape tomatoes to the pan and sauté for 2 or 3 minutes.

3) Add spinach and sauté until it is wilted to your liking

Bonus: Paleo Breads & Taco Shells

Paleo Backyard Hamburger Buns

Ingredients:
1) 3/4 cup almond flour
2) 1 tbsp flax seeds (optional)
3) 2 tbsp of psyllium seed powder
4) 2 large eggs
5) 1/2 cup coconut milk
*) 1 tsp baking powder
*) 1/2 tsp sea salt

Directions:
1) Preheat oven to 400 degrees F.
2) Mix almond flour, flax seeds, psyllium husks, sea salt and baking powder in a bowl.
3) Add eggs and coconut milk and mix carefully
4) Let it sit for 5 minutes
5) Cut the dough into 4 pieces, shape into buns and place on a parchment lined baking sheet
6) Bake for approx. 15 minutes
7) Remove from oven, allow to cool. Cut horizontally through center. Use to make your favorite paleo hamburger

Grain-free Sandwich Bread

Ingredients:
1) 1 cup smooth raw cashew butter at room temperature
2) 4 large eggs, separated (mine weighed about 9 ounces in their shells)
3) ¼ cup coconut flour
4) 2.5 teaspoons apple cider vinegar
5) ¼ cup almond milk
*) 1 teaspoon baking soda

*) ½ teaspoon sea salt
*) ½ to 2 tablespoons honey (use 2 tablespoons if you want it sweeter)Directions:

Directions:
1) Preheat your oven to 300 degrees. For a white colored loaf, place a small dish of water on the bottom rack.
2) Line the bottom of an 8.5×4.5 glass loaf pan with parchment paper, then spread a very thin coating of coconut oil on the sides of the pan.
3) With an electric mixer, beat the cashew butter with the egg yolks, then add the honey, vinegar, and milk.
4) Beat the egg whites in a separate bowl until peaks form
5) Combine the dry Ingredients: in another small bowl.
Note: Make sure your oven is completely preheated before adding the egg whites and the dry Ingredients: to the cashew butter mixture. You don't want your whites to fall, and the baking soda will activate once it hits the eggs and vinegar.
6) Pour the dry Ingredients: into the wet Ingredients:, and beat until combined. This will result in more of a wet batter than a dough. Make sure to get all of the sticky butter mixture off of the bottom of the bowl so you don't end up with clumps.
7) Pour the beaten egg whites into the cashew butter mixture, beating again until just combined. You don't have to be gentle with this, but don't over mix.
8) Pour the batter into the prepared loaf pan, then immediately put it into the oven.
9) Bake for 45-50 minutes, until the top is golden brown and a toothpick comes out clean. Do NOT open the oven door anytime before 40 minutes, as this will allow the steam to escape and you will not get a properly risen loaf.
10) Remove from the oven, then let cool for 15-20 minutes. Use a knife to free the sides from the loaf pan, then flip it upside down and release the loaf onto a cooling rack. Cool right-side up for an hour before serving.
11) Wrap the loaf up tightly and store in the fridge for up to 1 week.

Grain Free Taco Shells

Ingredients:
1) 3 ripe plantains
2) 1/2 cup avocado oil
3) 1 teaspoon freshly ground garlic sea salt (more if desired)
4) 1/2 teaspoon onion powder
5) Optional: 1 teaspoon (or more) hot sauce (like Cholula)
6) Optional: 1/2 lime squeezed

Directions:
1) Preheat oven to 350
2) Combine all Ingredients: in blender until they are pureed
3) On a parchment lined baking sheet space out sizable scoops of the puree
4) Using the back of a spoon spread out each scoop into a flat circle, about the size of your hand spread out flat
5) Bake for about 20 minutes, then flip them over for another 10 minutes until the "tortilla" becomes solid yet flexible
6) Remove baking sheet from oven and wait a minute for "tortillas" to slightly cool
7) Next "hang" each tortilla by folding it over a wire on the baking rack directly in the oven or use taco oven rack if you have one
8) Bake like this for another 20-30 minutes or until golden brown and crispy (center might be slightly more chewy depending on thickness and cooking time)
9) Remove from oven and prop them open while they cool slightly. If they cool closed, they are harder to fill with taco filling.
Note: Do not make tacos too thick in the center or they may crack easily. Keep them uniformly the same thickness.

BONUS: Paleo Desserts

Quick Chocolate Cherry Dessert

Ingredients:
1) 1 cup of cherries, fresh or defrosted
2) 1 teaspoon of cocoa powder
3) 1/8-1/4 cup shredded coconut

Directions:
1) Defrost your cherries, if they are frozen. If fresh, take the pits out.
2) Add your teaspoon of cocoa powder and thoroughly stir.
3) Add in your shredded coconut, until your desired amount.

No-Heat Pumpkin Pie Pudding

Ingredients:
1) 1/2 cup pumpkin puree
2) 2 tablespoons almond flour
3) 1/2 teaspoon pumpkin pie spice, or cinnamon/nutmeg
4) 1-2 tablespoons honey (to taste)

Directions:
1) Add your pumpkin puree to a small bowl or mug.
2) Add your almond flour and spices. Mix to incorporate.
3) Add 1 tablespoon of honey. Taste. Add another tablespoon if needed.

Chocolate Covered Frozen Banana and Peanut Butter Bites

Ingredients:

1) 3 medium-ripe bananas, sliced
2) 1/4 cup almond butter

3) 10 oz dark baking chocolate

Directions:
1) Arrange half of the banana slices on a baking sheet lined with parchment paper.
2) Spread bananas with almond butter.3) Top with the other half of banana slices and freeze for about one hour.
In the meantime,
4) Cut chocolate in pieces and put 2/3 of it in a microwave safe bowl. Microwave on medium power for 30 seconds, stir, then repeat in 15 interval until the chocolate has melted. (If you prefer to melt chocolate on the stove top, place a heatproof bowl over a small saucepan filled with simmering water. On low heat, stir chocolate until melted (allow a few minutes). Ensure the chocolate avoids contact with water and steam whilst melting).
5) Add 1/3 remaining chocolate and keep stirring until it is fully melted. This is called tempering chocolate. It will allow the chocolate to have a glossy texture and to set correctly.
6) Remove bites from the freezer and dip them into melted chocolate using two forks. Dip one bite at a time in melted chocolate and roll around to cover all sides. Using one fork, remove bite from chocolate. With the other fork, remove excess chocolate and arrange the bite back on baking sheet.
7) Freeze at least 3 hours or until ready to serve. Keep them in the freezer.

Paleo Watermelon Cake

Ingredients:
1) 1 large seedless watermelon
2) 2 cans full fat coconut milk (left in fridge for 6 hours or more)
3) 1 Tbsp. raw honey
4) 1 cup sliced almonds or shredded coconut
5) Sliced fresh fruit such as blackberries, strawberries and kiwi (for topping)
*) 1/2 tsp. vanilla extract

Directions:

Coconut whipped cream:

1) Place the can of coconut milk in the refrigerator for at least 6 hours (or overnight). This will cause the cream to separate from the milk. The cream will be at the top of the can.

2) Open the can of coconut milk and scrape out the cream into a medium sized bowl. (open the can from the bottom and pour the milk out into a separate container before scraping out the cream. Use the saved milk for smoothies and other recipes)

3) Add the vanilla and raw honey to the mixture.

4) Whip the cream with a hand mixer on medium speed and work your way up to high speed until the cream is fluffy, about 5 minutes (it will not be as fluffy as dairy whipped cream). Place the bowl of whipped cream in the fridge until ready to use.

Toasted almonds or coconut:

5) Place a medium sized skillet over medium-high heat and allow the pan to get hot.

6) Add the sliced almonds or shredded coconut and toss in the pan until they are toasted and turn a light brown color. Set aside to cool.

To assemble:

7) Remove the top and bottom from the watermelon and remove the rind from the middle section. You should be left with a cake-shaped piece of watermelon. Cut the watermelon "cake" into the number of wedges/slices you want. 6-8 slices is recommended depending on the size of the watermelon. Alternatively, you can leave the watermelon intact if you plan on traveling with it or do not want to cut it. Slicing a cake ahead of time makes it easier to dip the edges into the icing and then into anything else you want to adhere to the icing, such as the almonds or toasted coconut.

8) Pat the outside of the watermelon dry with paper towels.

9) Dip the outside edge of each slice into the coconut whipped cream and then into the toasted almonds or coconut, and reassemble the wedges into the cake shape on a serving platter. If you leave the watermelon whole, pat the whole thing dry before rolling the side in the coconut whipped cream.

10) Top with more whipped coconut cream and your favorite fresh fruit. Serve or store in the refrigerator until ready to serve.

Simple Banana Bread Muffins

Ingredients:
1) 2 cups almond flour
2) 3 eggs
3) 2 very ripe bananas
4) 1/4 cup coconut oil, melted
5) 2 teaspoons baking powder

Optional Add-ins:
*) 1 TBSP cinnamon
*) 1/2 cup chopped nuts
*) 1/2 cup dried fruit or fresh blueberries
*) 1/2 cup chocolate chips

Directions:
1) Preheat oven to 350 degrees.
2) This works best in the food processor but you can use a hand mixer too. Add the eggs, melted coconut oil and bananas to your bowl.
3) Blend until the bananas are completely mixed.
4) Add your almond flour and baking powder, and mix until fully incorporated.
5) Add your additional add-ins here if you are using any.
6) Pour into paper muffin liners in a regular muffin pan, or you can grease your muffin tin so the batter doesn't stick.
6) Cook at 350 for 18-25 minutes, until fully cooked and firm when you press on them.

Macadamia Chocolate Chip No-Heat Cookies

Ingredients:
1) 1 cup of macadamia nuts
2) 1 cup of shredded coconut
3) 1/4 cup of melted coconut oil
4) 1/4 cup of chocolate chips

5) 1 tablespoon of 100% pure maple syrup or honey

Directions:
1) Add nuts, shredded coconut, coconut oil and maple syrup or honey to a food processor.
2) Blend until relatively smooth, 1-2 minutes.
3) Fold in your chocolate chips.
4) Use a scoop and scoop out balls of the dough and flatten into cookie shapes
5) Put them in the fridge for at least 30 minutes to solidify

Super Easy Chia Pudding

Ingredients:
1) 1 (13.5oz) can coconut milk
2) 1/4 cup chia seeds
3) 1 tbsp. honey
4) 1 tsp. vanilla (optional)
5) 2 small mason jars (optional)

Directions:
1) Mix everything together and pour into mason jars or an airtight container.
2) Let it sit in the refrigerator overnight and enjoy it the next day topped with any fruit or nuts preferred.

Avocado Pear Popsicles

Ingredients:
1) 2 avocado
2) 2 pears (skin removed)

Directions:
1) Puree avocados and pears in a blender
2) Fill popsicle molds 3/4 full, insert sticks and freeze. (ice cube trays will work in a pinch)
3) Soak in hot water for a few seconds to remove the pops from the

mold.
4) Makes about six popsicles

Nectarine Kiwi Banana Baby Food Popsicles

Ingredients:
1) 3 nectarines
2) 1 kiwi (skin removed)
3) 2-3 inches of a banana

Directions:
1) Puree nectarines, kiwi and banana in a blender
2) Fill popsicle molds 3/4 full, insert sticks and freeze. (ice cube trays will work in a pinch)
3) Soak in hot water for a few seconds to remove the pops from the mold.
4) Makes about six popsicles

Mango Brûlée

Ingredients:
1) 2 fresh mangos
2) ¼ cup honey or 100% pure maple sugar
3) ⅛ teaspoon ground ginger
4) ¼ teaspoon ground cinnamon
5) pinch of ground nutmeg

Directions:
1) Turn on the broiler. Position the rack 6 inches below the heat source. Line a baking sheet with foil.
2) Cut through the mango on either side of the pit as evenly as possible.
3) In a small bowl, combine the remaining Ingredients: and brush on top of each mango slice. Place the mango slices on the prepared baking sheet. Make sure the mango halves are level so nothing drips off. If you need to, use crumpled tin foil to steady the mango.
4) Broil for 3 minutes, or until caramelized. Alternatively, you can

use a creme brûlée torch to caramelize the honey or 100% maple s
5) This is a fun and simple dessert. The same technique can be used on just about any fruit. Try peaches or bananas.

BONUS: Paleo Condiments

One Minute Mayo

Ingredients:
1) 1 egg yolk, room temperature
2) 1 tablespoon dijon mustard
3) 1 tablespoon water
4) 1 tablespoon lemon juice
5) 1 cup oil of choice

Directions:
1) Place egg yolk, mustard, water and lemon juice into a tall container.
2) Add your 1 cup of oil.
3) Using an immersion blender, place blade into bottom of your container. Turn on, and pump up and down a few times until everything is blender.
4) Season with salt & pepper, if desired. Store in the fridge.

Garlic Aioli (garlic flavored, mayo like dip or spread)

Ingredients:
1) 2 garlic cloves
2) 2 egg yolks
3) ½ to ¾ cup olive oil (depending on desired thickness)
4) Juice of ½ lemon
5) Pinch of salt

Directions:
1) Combine all Ingredients: except olive oil in a food processor or blender
2) Slowly add olive oil until the sauce is fairly thick
3. Dip with carrot fries

Dairy-Free Double Caramel Sauce

Ingredients:

1) 1/2 cup full fat coconut milk
2) 1/4 cup raw honey
3) 2 tbsp extra virgin coconut oil
*) Pinch of sea salt (optional)

Directions:
1) Mix all Ingredients: together in a small pot.
2) Turn the heat to high, whisking constantly.
3) Once the sauce comes to a boil lower the heat to medium.
4) Continue whisking constantly.
5) When the sauce begins to thicken, turn the heat to low.
6) The sauce is done when the color is light brown.
7) Take the pot off of the heat and pour the mixture into a bowl or container. Serve once cooled.
Note: Reheat if needed on a low setting in a pot on the stove.

Toasted Almond Hazelnut Butter

Ingredients:
1) 4 cups raw almonds (divided in 2)
2) 2 cups raw hazelnuts
3) 1/2 tsp sea salt
4) 2 whole vanilla beans, finely chopped

Directions:
1) Preheat oven to 350F
2) Place 2 cups of almonds and the 2 cups hazelnuts on a large baking sheet, making sure to keep them well separated so the nuts don't mix.
3) Toast in the oven for 15 minutes, moving the nut around a few times during the process.
4) Place the hazelnuts in a clean tea towel and close into a small bundle. Now hold the package in one hand and, with the other hand,

move the nuts around so that they grind against each other. Do this for a minute or so. When you open up the bundle, the hazelnuts will be totally skinless. Now carefully pick the nuts out, leaving the skins behind.

5) Add the toasted almonds, hazelnuts and raw almonds, as well as salt and chopped vanilla beans to the bowl of your food processor

6) Process for a total of about 20 minutes, stopping to scrape the sides from time to time, until the butter is very smooth and creamy and almost liquid in consistency. It will return to a firmer consistency once it's had a chance to rest and cool down.

7) Transfer to clean air tight glass jars or containers.

Avocado Pesto Sauce

Ingredients:

1) 1 ripe avocado
2) ½ cup fresh basil, tightly packed
3) 1½ Tablespoons fresh lemon juice (about 1 lemon)
4) ½ teaspoon minced garlic
5) ¼ teaspoon sea salt, or more to taste

Directions:

1) Add the fresh basil, lemon juice and garlic into a mini food processor, and process until the basil is broken down a bit
2) Add the flesh of the ripe avocado, the ¼ teaspoon of sea salt and process again until smooth and creamy, stopping to scrape down the sides, as necessary
3) Taste the pesto, and adjust seasonings, if necessary
4) Serve over pasta or veggies.

Sugar Free Sweet and Sour Sauce

Ingredients:
1) 1/2 cup apricot preserves (no sugar added)
2) 1/3 cup coconut aminos

3) 1 tablespoon apple cider vinegar

Directions:
1) Whisk all Ingredients: in a small saucepan and bring to a boil
2) Lower heat and whisk for a few minutes. For an extra-thick sauce, whisk at medium heat for a few minutes more. The sauce will thicken as it cools
3) Serve with vegetables, poultry, or meat

Worcestershire Sauce

Ingredients:
1) 1/2 cup apple cider vinegar
2) 2 tbsp coconut aminos
*) 1/4 tsp ground ginger
*) 1/4 tsp mustard powder
*) 1/4 tsp onion powder
*) 1/4 tsp garlic powder
*) 1/8 tsp cinnamon
*) 1/8 tsp freshly ground black pepper
*) 2 tbsp water

Directions:
1) Combine all the Ingredients: in a saucepan and slowly bring to a boil while stirring frequently.
2) Let simmer for about a minute for the flavors to develop.
3) Cool and store in the refrigerator.

Everyday Mustard

Ingredients:
1) 1/2 cup mustard powder
2) 1 tablespoon of white wine vinegar
*) 1/2 cup water
*) Pinch of chopped fresh parsley or basil, lemon or lime zest (optional)
*) Sea salt to taste

Directions:
1) Combine the mustard powder and water in a bowl and mix well.
2) Add water slowly until has a creamy mustard-like consistency
3) Let the mustard stand for about 15 minutes before enjoying. Store refrigerated in an air-tight container

Whole-grain mustard

Ingredients:
1) 1/4 cup yellow mustard seeds
2) 1/4 cup brown mustard seeds
3) 1 cup white wine or water
4) 4 tsp mustard powder
5) 1/4 white wine vinegar
*) 1/2 tsp sea sal

Directions:
1) Soak the mustard seeds in the white wine or water overnight.
2) Place the seeds and soaking liquid in a blender or food processor with the mustard powder, vinegar and sea salt. Process to a paste consistency.
3) Put in a glass jar, cover and refrigerate for about 4 days before serving.

Cajun Creole Spicy Mustard

Ingredients:
1) 1 cup mustard seeds
2) ½ cup white wine vinegar
3) ½ lemon, juiced
4) 1 tsp ZATARAIN'S® Creole Seasoning (adjust to taste)
*) ½ cup water (add last)
*) Sea salt & pepper, to taste (optional)

Directions:
1) Mix together all Ingredients: in a food processor or blender

2) Add water slowly until has a creamy mustard-like consistency
3) Let the stand for about 15 minutes before serving. Store refrigerated in an air-tight container

Homemade Ketchup

Ingredients:
1) ½ cup, plus 2 tablespoons tomato paste
2) ¼ cup raw honey
3) ½ small onion
4) 1 garlic clove
5) ⅓ cup apple cider vinegar
*) ¾ teaspoon fine grain sea salt
*) 3) ⅓ cup water

Directions
1) Using a food processor or blender, puree garlic and onion until smooth.
2) In a medium saucepan over medium heat, combine: tomato paste, honey, water, apple cider vinegar, salt, garlic and onion. Whisk until very smooth and bring to a boil.
3) Reduce heat to low and let gently simmer for 20 minutes, stirring every so often. The sauce will thicken and the flavors will bind.
4) Remove from the heat, cover with a lid and let cool at room temperature. Once cool, transfer to an airtight container and keep in the fridge.

Thank you again for purchasing this book. If you enjoyed any of the recipes here, please go back to where you bought this book from and leave a review.

Alec Sommers

The End.

Printed in Great Britain
by Amazon